The Essence of a MESMERIZING EARTH

Q.B. WINGFIELD

Copyright © 2017 by Quyionah Wingfield
Book design by Inkstain Design Studio

All rights reserved. No part of this publication may be reproduced, distributed, or transmitted in any form or by any means, including photocopying, recording, or other electronic or mechanical methods, without the prior written permission of the publisher, except in the case of brief quotations embodied in critical reviews and certain other noncommercial uses permitted by copyright law.
For permission requests, write to the publisher, addressed "Attention: Permissions Coordinator," at the address below.

JazzElle Publishing
2897 N. Druid Hills Road Ste 202
Atlanta, GA 30329
www.jazzellepubliahing.com

Ordering Information:
Quantity sales. Special discounts are available on quantity purchases by corporations, associations, and others.
For details, contact the publisher at the address above.

Orders by U.S. trade bookstores and wholesalers.
Please contact Ingramspark: by visiting www.ingramspark.com.
Printed in the United States of America

Contents

ART, SHAPE ME

A Mile Through My Soliloquy
What's in My Soul
Hip-Hop (Rockin' Don't Stop)
Pain Builders Pain Killers
Dr. Gordon's Park
New Beginnings
Sarah's Dance
I.A.S.M.

WORLD OF TATTOOS

I'm Going Crazy (Am I?)
This is life
World of Tattoos
Soldiers
Get it How I Live
Child Support (An Ode to Single Mothers)

LOSS

Inner Soul Speaking
Purity Murderer
Not Enough
Am I to Just Be Okay?
Samsonite Man
Tainted Souls

SAPIOSEXUAL

Intellectual High
Tale of the Fateful Fall
This Game
Selfish Love
Path of Choice (Mr. Right VS Mr. Wrong)
Dimensional Speaking

LOVE OF MY LIFE

Forever
Goodbye Lust Hello Love
Nothing More to Say
Forever After
Unlisted Clouds of Love
Jaira

ONE WITH NATURE

Nature
You Are Who I Choose
Outside

APPRECIATION FOR LIFE

Inspiration Comes Through You
Spiritual Young Woman
Sound Body, Sound Mind

SELF-REFLECTION

Sleep
Virgo's Loneliness
Reverie Dream
Destination
Confidence
Empty Meets Free
Love is to Blame, Faith is its Dame
The God Within
Athena
The Essence of a Mesmerizing Earth

AFFIRMATIONS

Gratitude

Collaboration

Cup Full of Openness

Unconditional Love and Regard

Attitude of Gratitude

Virtues of Joy

All I Do is Win

Honor Thyself

Managing Karma

Self-Preservation is Peace

Yoga and Meditation

I Love Myself

Learn to Let It Go

Moral Compass

Sunshine

Relationship with Peace

Self-Love

The Essence of a MESMERIZING EARTH

Art,
SHAPE ME

A Mile Through My Soliloquy

It never entered my mind
I'd fall in love so easy
It's about that time
I walk **Miles Ahead**
When **Autumn Leaves**
Birthed Cool
Moon Dreams
Taking seven steps to the **heaven of my soul**
When I'm feeling **Kind of Blue**
Drinking love
Straight, No Chaser
All of him
Soothes the whole of me
Bye, Bye Blackbird
My Funny Valentine
Sketched Flamingo kisses across my heart

I could write a book

Of all the **Perfect Ways**

He touches me

Near and far

Should I indulge or retreat **Round Midnight**

Basin Street Blues

Is my reverie

Shall I live and be free

Or wake from my **mile**-long daydream

What's in My Soul

craziness in calm
dancing souls linger on
shell immobile but strong
creativity forever

visionaries
on a bridge of happiness
parading arms
and legs
swaying in grace
kissing perfection

a design
only naturalism
makes understandable
to its own kind
fearless dreams

dancing in
pouring down rain

pained
burnt feet
a sweet taste of
remaining forever

moments articulating stories
of perspective and perception

arms and legs in a serene display
I can create
ANYTHING and EVERYTHING
as I'm
DANCING forever

Hip-Hop (Rockin' Don't Stop)

Rick James Jamz

with Mary J and lets go

James Brown & Rakim

uses their Souls

Kendrick Lamar gets out of Control

and Everyone's Infatuated

with The Love Below

I have no Doubt Reason will flow through blue Jays

prophesize the World as Yours

till the end of our days

Nastradamus sees lives that are Supa Dupa Fly

Miss me

Missy

Lil Weezyana will never die

Go DJ

Grandmaster Flash The Fury of 5

Queen B's sting is hardcore when she Flashes her Light

The West coast Rubix Cube's shine like Diamonds Forever

And the cops in L.A. trip

N.eva W.ork A.lone stick together

Life gets overwhelming

and I Daydream about Fiascos

I need a Drink to ease me from all the Pain that I walk through

On top of that I have to get rid of my old boo for my new boo

I'm like Monie in the Middle soon to be chopped and screwed

I'm poppin' Eminem's trying to get some Flava Flav

Public Enemy number one

Life's prices drive me insane

At the end of the day

there's much me and the world have in Common

That we're living in multiple anomalies

Of transformational logic

In this World called Hip-Hop I'm lost in love

I'd die without it

Pain Builders Pain Killers

will well weld well
a still spell
spills where we dwell
heaven hails sound of bells
and still I see me fail
inner critic giving up the will to be well

seas sway she said
simply have empathy
warmth love and sincerity
cure my dis-ease, leave sympathy
amend my sea leaves to see my destiny

quick time trips prime
dips fine but find a line
don't drown in the

present pleasant peasant
hell in heaven
11 to 7
today's hopeful mission and tomorrow's painful lesson

indoctrinate my inclination to debate
lies
me they infuriate
not using my great
looking for refuge, I pray
For the day I raise
my supreme being to emulate
not 10% but 100% of
love

Dr. Gordon's Park

A visual artist and his camera.

Dr. Gordon
Parks
His eyes on a wave
A small child
Wiping her eyes of yesterday
Viewing life's detail
Grandma's graceful watchful gaze on the stoop
Seems stressed
But how blessed to be stressed
With trial and error for growth
Snap, snap
The craft of shaft was just half
Of the vision
Dr. Gordon's soaring visionary

Park

It is an enchanting forest
Of real life
Sun sets in shades of oranges and blues
Waterfalls on a vocal moon
While the crack on the concrete moves
Mother black, rose
From the street to be a wholesome Queen
And that grass grows so long
So strong
Reflections of a King
Shining in the rain
All the pain he's sustained
The picture taken in his mind
Tells the perfect story every time
Lifting trash off the corner
And completing a scripted puzzle
That no one can see
Grandma's aged hands
Tell the story of
Life
Happiness
Pain
Work
Gain
Through each line

Most eyes refined
But Dr. Gordon's Park
Displays the in and out of
Multi-dimensional melaninated life

New Beginnings

Salutations

I know y'all been through a creative starvation,

but Athena here

with a mental penetration.

A new creation

to make your body feel vibrations

I have much consideration

For starving babies

trying to make their gravy.

But all this blarney must be interrupted

In love, we must trust

It's left up to us

To make music back harmonious

So, I'm gone have to obliterate

All you generating hate

You're infuriated perpetrated

Babies made

In this fake industry race

And its mayday

To silence your imprudent ways

Your clear negative rays

There's so much to say

I'm holding on like I've been mistaken

There ain't no changing?

What about the street gangs

And maybe the music stages

Stop being reality T.V. entertainers

Teach the babies how to build conglomerations

Build a stronger nation

I see the grass can be greener

We need more Kings more Queens

Representing like Obama and Nzinga

More compatible

Not perpetuating negatives and clones

NEW BEGINNINGS

Anything goes with your foes

Beguiling not the way to roll

Secrets like Toni Braxton

In my face, I see the facts roll in

That we need to stop acting

And get it crackin, poppin, pumpin come on

Join me on this new beginning

Let's start something

Sarah's Dance

"Sarai! Noble Princess"

Dancing

Through the midst of karmic days

Talking to God

Amazed

How she birthed new ways

With her geisha like gaze

Traveling through time

Sitting with Nzinga

Creating a strategy to

Humble the young

Not so great Alexander

Time travels

Through Sarah's dance

She stops to decode

Da Vinci's lonely heart

Substance remaining the quest
Internal metamorphosis
Of life is what she teaches
Drinking green tea with Nostradamus
As she explains how words hold power
Speak and you shall see
Calamity and peace upon your visions
Premonitions and intuition
Just let your heart laugh in the moments of now
Breathe with the stars
See, Sarah dances guidance into all of our hearts
Departing with a heart full of gold
Daughter of the heavens birthed by Terah
Sarah dances with the world
Walking through time portals
The sister, daughter, and wife
enchanting little girl
Dancing grace into our hearts
Birthing a better world

In a Sentimental Mood

The Mountain Top

Wind Talking

Two Beings Breathing

In A Sentimental Mood

Standing on the Bridge of Harmony

Looking at the Stars for Peace

Of Mind

Vaughan, Coltrane and Ellington

Playing the Melody of Love

In A Sentimental Mood

Lovers Swim in Calmness

Alarmed by the Connection

The Water and our Daughters Centered

Peace and Tranquility

This is how we breathe

Oh, How We Live

In A Sentimental Mood

Congruent hearts that appreciate each other

Meditation on the rock

late nights any weather

The park is our center where we enter

Heaven Finding our LOVE

In A Sentimental Mood

"I think it's better that I tell you now."

Making Love Playing Jill

Perfection is less than perfect

But in human experience we penetrate depth

In A Sentimental Mood

Suns rising and setting

We're never forgetting

That God and Earth aligned us to be

With each other

Souls meeting in Love

"He's so sweet and good, good. I can't let him go."

Pure Heaven…. Ah……Love

In A Sentimental Mood

World of
TATTOOS

I'm Going Crazy (Am I?)

Change going on in this life
Feel I'm the only one who sees
Women killing their babies
Grown men kindergarten cravings
Emotions creating poverty more everyday

Sometimes I cry at night
Living in a land of "we gone be alright"
Women don't stick together
Gangs killing code started by our ancestors
Feeling like death this can't be life

Anorexia is the ideal state
And we all seem to be grown at eight
They create the plan to make us fight
Sunken in a mentality of stationary life

Conditional love is our dividing epidemic

Religion
False preachers
Internal peace
Child's mind destroyed through affirmed hate
Before they can even speak
Take facts away
So, we can't learn
Get mad when their kids follow our words
This is life the illusions
We now see through them

This is Life

The star shines with light beams as her shadow
As the baby looks out the window
Learning her path

Stating an August Virgo
With a smile out of the ghetto
This queen grows up fast

Sweet hummingbirds give her a tone to remember
When money stops flowing
When mommy's eyes are black and blue in the winter

Please don't hit her, Athena screams under her breath
Loose change we had to work with
Baby eyes at mommy, *where do we go next?*

Not another need to complain

Cause complaining don't produce change
The days and nights no lights
Positive and what not, this is life

Ruff tuff Jersey in our veins
No matter the problem still engage
Instilled with rage
Dwelling in programming's cage
The struggle the fight
Through it all
For some, this is life

World of Tattoos

Watch this chain of command
No freedom still clutching hands
Their views separating life
Overshadow love with lust and lies
Thoughts fall, fly
As I ask myself why
Why are we dependent
On what others think we should be?
I see there's so much to prove
There's so much to lose
I'm standing out in this world of tattoos
I have to rely on me to make my life fulfilling
You can choose what you want to choose
But I watered my apple tree
I don't want to be you

It's hard to be or achieve
When change negatively
Redefines happiness in life
But I will fight
Against anything I don't feel is right
To prove I won't be moved
By this world of tattoos

World of tattoos
World of tattoos
I am not a part of you
Mind over matter
When faith starts to shatter
Rhetoric will try to cloud the truth
But I ain't scared of this world of tattoos

Soldiers

Gossipers and haters
Are no better than terrorists
Killing images of their prey
In need of mental bliss

Gay is bad
Women-shaming exists
Kiss goodbye happiness
Cause they'd rather slander
While Miranda Rights are being dissed

They fight and the kids get the punishment
Vote or die, then to the war we're sent
So I say, If you really want to be free
Take a stance just like me and in each other let's believe

Soldiers, you gotta fight for what's in your heart

Soldiers, don't let hatred take the part
Soldiers, this is your life do what you want to

The world won't change
You have to engage
In the peace in you

Get It How I Live

Question:

Why do you stand in the corner of your mind?
Every day with your baggy jeans privilege on
Not aware that your life can be gone
Eliminated at any moment
Eternally stagnant back and forth into poverty's jail
Destined for doomsday

Answer:

My freedom was questioned
The moment I took my first breath
Out of the womb
Criticize and chastise me as the cord was cut loose
Because I don't fit the census

Oxygen pure in my veins
But I'm living in this cell you call life
In the likes of stifling pride
Vicariously living through our dis-eased ancestors
But even when we learn the lesson
We're still treated as less than

Question:

Why do you need to indulge in
Whatever you consider to be survival?
To gain money or prosperity
Draining love and long-term strategy
Your choice makes you your own rival
Yet you find it vital
To stick to this script
Why is this?

Answer:

My rebuttal to the madness
They tend to call blackness
Is that I AM a black man
They claim there's a gun is in my hand
Then take the opportunity to distribute the land

My body's property value
Is undervalued
Young and growing trying to build a plan
To dig my feet out of the sand
Try to live with skin like mine
It's hard to find
Ordinary circumstances that allow peace from 9 to 5
Per the American dream
The closer I am to my culture
The further away I am from wealth
But other cultures thrive on appropriating me
and branding it as themselves
Conformists act as if they're blind
Inclined
Not to help my kind
Enduring like Huey vicariously living through
Blacks Practicing Freedom
Edge of the coloring book I'm way out of line
Hacking pink elephants and distorted declines
Achieve greatness?
Not when I need to
Practice insanity to meet the quota
Provocative cruise ships forgetting I'm God
I must act as my life is made up of
Next door street hustling is not my dream
Extravagant games of inferiority I can't cling

onto

Sustaining my family is a need
And starving is not my bid
So, thru all this I'm stating
I'm left to get it how I live

Child Support
(An Ode to Single Mothers)

Where is my child's support?

Can my child get his support?

Why are you amazed with enragement?

Because I ask for my child's support?

When you and I were necessary you did anything and

everything imaginable

just to appease your thoughts of my love for you.

When you got a chance to stick it through,

tears of joy climaxed from you

exclusivity in a non-traditional bond

prompted the validity

that you were ready and thought it through.

Now attachments are available,

this email you pushed off like it was a virus dude.

A seed coming to see with his life

what variations of substance we can pursue.

When he enters

you exit

as if he's a peasant

not allowed to be in your presence.

You come back every election

CHILD SUPPORT (AN ODE TO SINGLE MOTHERS)

to make the correction

I love my child

thoughts of him loving another man you get vexed.

I cannot ask you for a real thing,

just some money and maybe a fling

but this is not a preference

I would like to explore the possibilities of.

Why does he have to suffer?

Because you won't make him supper.

Expect me to muster up

What I can to play the puppet.

I'm at your cubicle doing your job,

took my serenity with words of love.

Now you hold no debt to me

though you tricked me

into believing that this was a WE thing.

I was too naive to know the sting of third degree.

You're scared

I'm left with the notion to create motion

to do for who's in need

so he can eat.

The notion of you taking

one day to care for yours,

you're a day care with limited hours.

Forget the state

Forget who hates

They weren't there when you begged him not to leave.

Now that my child has been conceived

and he's the one deceived,

you should know

support of his father is what he'll need.

CHILD SUPPORT (AN ODE TO SINGLE MOTHERS)

Inner Soul Speaking

Another somber love song
Pretend there's nothing on
My soul's footprint is so oblong
That I can't hide who I am

How can I sit and think of myself?
My life a core of my lens
But not use the passion
I must help for better health

The burdens I feel
Wake up to night lights like I've been killed
Premonitions of the future
If I don't help
It feels like I've killed them myself

Being so young and feeling someone else's pain
Next to them without a name
But see their whole life in one blink
Damn
How do you think I feel?

I see the glass the cracked pipes
And I see the poverty in most minds
And I know that I am one of many
who could shed some light
But as a human being
I feel restricted
In having such a burden over my life

Even though I've lived a truthful life
It would be the biggest lie
To let the time go by
And think just because only you and God know the sacrifice
That you're not supposed to live what you promised, right?
What you promised from your past life
That you'd make a difference and emulate the source of Free life
Emulate the plan to get the earth right
Why are you playing games with people lives?

Purity Murderer

Falling into categories

Prisoners

Perpetrators

Unwilling debaters

See it's a shame

It's a mockery

When it's time to have their back

They lack tenacity

Bloody hands

Murdering

What's pure what's sane because it's naive

Let me gift you

you'll have more of me

The facts of doubt

Makes these terms of murder insanity

Love becomes the alibi

For her to accept and cry

Out tears of uncertainty

talking clever
in good weather
Then create bad
whether
It harms or not
because his charm
charmed the hearts
of many pure lives of naivete
She was watching sweet sixteen
At prom he danced to Billie Jean
Stop has no meaning
He's lost she's lost
Still no reason for treason
The mockery
just off the bottle
Now he's skating
Robbing cradle dreams
Boy of mystery
Is really a man
gone to murder more purity

PURITY MURDERER

Not Enough

Take is all that he seems to do
Then I break constantly into two
Cause what he makes me feel
when I'm on misty blue
Is that I need his love

The signs were there
How speedy of me
I was blind
In love immediately
He made me sigh
I couldn't clear the debris
He was all I could think of

He takes my heart
Away from me
I'm trying to clear the smog

So I can see
He holds me close
So I can't breathe
Can't seem to break from the hold
I can't take it no more

I am strong
But it feels like it's not enough
Moving from what's wrong
Still it's not enough
He holds me
Controls my everything
One day I'll move along
But now I feel that
I don't have enough

Am I To Just Be Okay?

As smart as I believed myself to be
That's just how naïve I was
To think his love
Was unconditional and sincere
I thought I was smarter than the other ones
Thought I'd peep game
But my heart was played with just for fun
He wasn't the same
Played with my purity
Life all about him and me
I'm here all alone
The script he wrote was sold
How bold of him to fold
"I love you, I love you"
"I want us to be together"
Now it's forget me

Who's B?

I can choose to care whenever

What do I do?

When he's sporadically in my life

Am I supposed to say that's alright?

When I cried at night

Do I erase?

The hurtful deceit

The pain that embodied thee

I'm stuffed

Damn how much can I eat

My happiness on the line

A hello without hate

Am I to just be okay?

Samsonite Man

He comes and goes
No one knows
What to say
When he's on his way
When he's home it's good
Hold it down like a real man should
But at the blink of an eye
Samsonite's gone with no goodbye
Fretful is left me
The feeling oh so bittersweet
Cause when I'm open
He changes position
And I'm sitting there empty
He's gone
I'm hurt and move on with my time
Living a comfortable life

Now everything's fine
Then he comes back with old news
Comes to rendezvous
He's that suave sexy debonair cat
That swiftly moves ya heart with tact
And each time he leaves and comes back
I still trust that he'll stay
I believe dat
While I'm patiently waiting
We're constantly fornicating
With no validation
There's a future in the making
And I'm trying to formulate
This false state
Of him and I so engagingly together
But when the seasons change
September/May
He's back on his way
Damn, what more can I say?
But I can't help but be smitten with him
Because the time spent is so heavenly
The love he's given me
Becomes a drug I can't get rid of
Samsonite
Next time you have your luggage ready
Prepare me

Cause then I'll have the strength to say
No tomorrow goodbye today

Tainted Souls

Perception dictates reality
I'm here but I'm not
Fear what is hot
But cold turn the soul from passion, loves block
Ether gleams then she's gone
Love or lust which in the song
But we all sing along
La la la, la la la

Diligent demons
Spreading their treason
Creating cement, blocking the reason
We're here in the 1st place
But we still say
La la la, la la la

Bombs blaring, curtains closing

People chose to, put their nose in
Sing "war huh" we rock side to side
La la la, la la la

Baby born in cluttered womb
Before his third eye opened
Prepared a way, made his tomb
The block is hot, barred home soon
Mama sang
La la la, la la la

Crash course collision
No envisioning Stevie's vision
Children are given no home to live in
Just a roof over head
Love forbidden, they say
Ha ha ha, ha ha ha

Someday there has to be
A place for replenished souls
Fulfilling the art of love
Finding fullness as free
Beings
Singing their song of
ah ah ah, ah ah ah

Sapiosexual

Intellectual High

Visions categorizing

this new horizon

The slant of the oak

Projects this mixture

Of noise and silence

Creativity of our minds

Meant conceptions

Correcting any indecent vexed messages

My internal sensation alert

Deserving peace from treason

That has beamed in

Eliminated from knowing my worth

Stating my beauty by looking me in my eyes while speaking

Making love with your mind

I want it everyday

Even on the weekend

Your voice tantalizing

kMy ears

The pressure

The new position

God sent you to analyze my mind

You've got mine

Complete mission

Lucky me no mask no disguise

Oh, but a high that I don't want to decline don't want to see its demise

This drug is not burning my brain it's freeing my mind

Rendezvous

I'm on a continuous rise

Thank you for this intellectual high

Tale of the Fateful Fall

Heavy waves tremble my skin
As my faith runs thin
You were always here
when the wind would talk too loud
The rain falls from my eyes
Your hands use to shield my cry
Now I'm all alone
In a world so cold
As I begin to unfold
The untold
Pain
ripping through my veins.
My memories of you will help me stay strong
happiness venturing along
Reminded me of me
What I used to be at three

Inhibited free
In love with all that life had to bring
Tale of the fateful fall
Tale of the faithful fall
And the God in you protected my heart from it all

This Game

I want you to love me

but don't want you to love me.

You're in love with me

but love is so tricky.

Love, I'm full of it

or am I full of that sticky.

I do but I don't know,

Where am I?

I move swiftly.

So, I

stop and try

to gain my composure.

To give my all to you

what you deserve ten times over.

You change ya position

a ball game my first miss

and I'm back to square one

aware

of the tear, my heart's living.

I think is it karma

or just drama

taking my hand.

I want what's new

I felt the truth

now I don't understand.

Fiddle de fiddle

It's left

me in the middle,

my shot

and I just dribble

flip flop

trying not to miss you.

I thought this love thing

was something I needed,

to help me grow past

this power struggling.

Now I'm open and soaking

becoming love's fiend,

this game is taking a major toll on me.

Selfish Love

cynical and blue
average and looking for clues
heart on a rampage
for meaningful praise
appreciation for love and life
sonority made the day

Brooklyn's question
i ask the sun, blind
love, love me
with endless intrigue and surprise

no hide away for a better day
no tide away for a sleepless lay
cause tomorrow is promised only to sun rays

i want to have your forever and ever

i will appreciate you through mo betta and countless endeavors
ask me am I clever
to ask for your love when she's close
ask me am I clever
to expect me as the one you love most

solace
catch 22's recline
the hurtful demise
of you and I
substantial lives
mocked my beguiled soul
for happiness is a part
of my meaningful guy
peace I will leave with
as we live separate lives

SELFISH LOVE

Path of Choice
(Mr. Right vs. Mr. Wrong)

One man represents
everything that is right.
The other man represents
everything that is wrong.
Comfort lies in what's wrong,
discord travels with what is right,
not sure if conditioning is walking her down the aisle
of destruction,
or if the feeling with Mr. Wrong
Is actually all that's right.
In the end
She chooses herself.
Tumultuous and lonely
but the reward and discomfort of reconditioning
shows that the decision
was for the best.

To recondition her soul
For a pure walk, down love's road.

Dimensional Speaking

the decency of my sensuality
a musical composition
played out by a symphony
playing my measurements
my feet
my land
my thighs
the tip of my forehead
a sweet kiss of my sky
exploring me in and out
what you can see in
what can come out
the tongue the mouth
one of life's most precious treasures
what does yours measure
an artist, doctor, or a competitor

can you explore?
am I talking about
sex, love, music or all the above?
whispers capturing tones
vibration leveraged
motionless
my third dimension
makes me a supreme Earth
that I can make a believer
out of a deceiver
turn a pessimist
into a faithful love dealer
we see the grotesque normality
speeches of informal formality
reason must begin
in this life of harsh fallacies
touching vague stages of
what's called sexuality
make you look for the real reality

Love of
MY LIFE

Forever

Darling if I could
Darling then I would
Spend my all of my nights
With you forever

And Baby, if I decide
To escape the world divide
You I would confide in forever

I would see the sun with you
Every night and every day
My day bright green
No more feeling blue
Because I'm with you babe

You brighten the seasons of my heart
Make me smile so heavenly

Your eyes are like antique art
And forever with you I'll be

It enlightens me
To see you love the way you do
Every day I see God work through you

You're my heartbeat
Always in tune
With the truth
Serenity lives in you

FOREVER

Goodbye Lust Hello Love

The inner visions
Of false love's imprisonment
It's so hard not to cry

Change has divided
Me between my inner peace
And relying on you trying to hard

Love set me free
To feel alive
I know I can be free when I let go of belief and pride

Lust, I am no longer in your chain of fools
You will not rake me along
I'm not to be used

No more crying
No more relying
I'm flying to love

Shallow is no longer a part of my thesis
Now that lust has swam away
I can pick up love's pieces

Nothing More to Say

Follow me
So, we can flee
Not to a fairyland
But where our love can land
And be all in

Clouds may show
Us days we just don't know
But if you trust in me
In heaven, we will be endless friends

Brooklyn knows
What's best for your heart
So, I'll show you a jazzy way to play the part
I'm playing it smart
No Rolling Stones here's my actions

I'll give you my love and that's your satisfactions

Don't dress for me
I want your divinity
I love who you are inside
So, baby don't hide
It from me

Soul to soul
No heartache to heartbreak
We're two whole people
But we'll make mistakes
Here's my gratitude
A new me I introduce
Not fearful of our amalgamation of plays
I'll show you my cards
So, there's nothing more to say

Forever After

be my prince charming
make my heart a ray
let my spirit swim in bliss
of your intelligent light days
be my ocean floor
my ever after more
that makes my heart shine in the dark
a heart that shines the light of love's soar
you are the light that blocks the clouds
and makes my smile sing out loud
for your love is not arrogant nor too proud
but a love that sings the songs of life's most elegant sounds
be the precious eyes that make my tears of joy
show me your inner spirit, a man from a boy
be my kiss in the evening
be that intelligence so intriguing
my companionship through all seasons

be my godly greeting
be my heaven love
a warm hug
be my earth laughter
and if one day
you may
love me forever after

Unlisted Clouds of Love

Tender kisses wash away all blemishes

noise and sound from a distance.

Time slow, body shivering

eyes glistening

getting brighter and brighter.

Light seems to get lighter and lighter.

You believe it's that scrape on your knee

from previously fighting it.

You shake, shake hard

when things go wrong.

You use that as a reason to leave it alone.

You think it's a scratch, move or a new zone.

Our representatives conversing as us on the phone

No,

It's that massage you get in your head, when you think

about it in bed.

The light is green and you feel its comfortable hug

then before this kiss is over you realize it's love.

Jaira

At that time, I was ready to go
Then God sent you right to me
Breaking down was my lonely soul
But then Jaira came to save me
Confused lost a day full of regret
Cause my life wasn't mine not yet
Opinions, should you stay should you leave
I choose life cause without you there's no need for me
My soul lost I can no longer breathe
Still not fully accepting of me
Felt your touch and it overwhelmed my heart
I've fallen in love
Can a human being be more precious more beautiful?
To just make my quest to exude passion easier
Such an inspiration, genuine love you made me a believer
A diva, a star is born, see to the world
You'll be amazing, have the world craving your gifts

To mommy you're a blessing, an inspiration for progression
For me my very best friend
My angel straight from heaven
Ms. Jazzelle I thank you
For changing my life
And inspiring me to be better

Jaira Jazzelle

One

WITH NATURE

Nature

I am a bird

flying through

cool waters of the ocean.

A tree reaching

777

singing with the wind

telling a new story.

I am a cheetah

running fast

in the hot heat

of a glistening moon.

A baby all alone in a doctor's room,

feeling air after leaving the womb,

with 100% of her mind active.

I am the wind guiding the clouds,

to someone's destiny of peace.

A piano, a trumpet, a voice, a roar

Robert, Miles, Amy, Malcolm

God takes over every time.

Nature,

I am a force of nature,

Naturally I am pure at heart

In my place of comfort and peace

I am nature

You Are Who I Choose

I take all my thoughts of you
and stretch them over my body.
You become my inner beauty
the substance
no one could take from me.
I feel the pressure,
the adrenaline
creeping in.
This discrete
Determination,
releasing aggravation.
Chills trickling,
your essence relieves me from mental anguish.
I hope this feeling will never leave,
no matter who or what deceives,
annunciates their greed.

I'll have no reason to need,

anyone else.

From you

I become a woman with never-ending

spiritual wealth,

mental health,

physical self.

Intense sensational pleasure,

my body tingles from this treasure,

flesh of my flesh

feels good

but they can never measure.

You're irreplaceable amid endless my endeavors.

Never feeling the blues of who is who,

It is you that I breathe

Air

you are who I choose.

Outside

sky lights up
soft breeze
wind
breathing and whispering

trees still
at a slant
sleeping
grass gliding
hair risen
from the wind's beautiful voice

stars analyzing
their match way under

clouds walk
soft and slow

like a baby
setting history
making its mark

beauty of the cat
stop to make eye contact
claiming its queen stability

the small insects make their way
around for food to return to their families

I sit on the steps
present with each
smiling graciously
with pleasure and serene moments
of a shell being a catalyst between
nature
soul
body
and mind

live in the midst of outside

Appreciation
FOR LIFE

Inspiration Comes Through You

?Vertigo?

The state I dare to be released from

This will open me up to pure Nirvana

Equanimity

Peace

Love

Equality

Do I deserve the spiritual freedom?

When I antagonize my spirit with impure actions

How can I annunciate

That my intentions are not to fabricate

But really live without hate

And cleanse my all in your refuge

I'll take refuge

And hope that my impurity is eradicable

That because of you I live to treat each living being as my equal

That because of you I become a living form of virtue

Through all three eyes I see the light

As a being of sin, I may wander off

But inclined in me is truth

My proof is the air I breathe

In my soul

I grow within my virtue of mental prudence

Pure inspiration comes through you

Spiritual Young Woman

(IN RESPECTS TO MAYA ANGELOU'S
"PHENOMENAL WOMAN")

Flaunting my smile from sunset to rise
Prayerful grace catching love's sublime eye
What you see is just a pinch of my inside
Because I am a spiritual young woman

Sista don't discredit me because you desire my approval
Don't make your vibe anal and conceited because my subtle style you're not used to
You too can have your own
If you learn to love all that you do
And I still love you
because I'm a spiritual young woman

Don't think because my age limits drinks
That I'm not an intellectual
And because my jeans fit just right
Means you're not an imposter of my physical
What you want, need to have, simply because it's biblical?
No Papi, you need time with God to talk with my soul
Cause I'm a spiritual young woman

I desire meditation over updating my Facebook pages
When I ask you what you want you're hurt
My concern for you is debated
My love for you is genuine, I'm seeking to also understand my impulses and cravings
It's because I'm a spiritual young woman

So, when you see me try not to overthink
You'll go too far
Just let your conscience breathe
The spirit heals coded scars
Neither envy nor blasphemy to my four mothers I forever learn more
Lady O, Nzinga, Teresa, and Maya, this spiritual young woman will continue to soar

Sound Body, Sound Mind

Humble surroundings
Enlightened profoundness
Love on the way to heaven
Future grounded
Oneness crowned
With positivity
Time given
Stability
Serenity
Direction
Positivity
Negativity dropped off behind
Fulfillment
Of my sound body sound mind

Time traveling

The mind-channeled

Sing

I am at the core of my happiness

Consistently handling

The Unknown of what the future brings

At peace with my inner spirit

I believe I am the dream

I surpass the state of sleep

I am God

God is me

Clarity is what to bring

You have to believe

In your sound mind sound body

Self-REFLECTION

Sleep

I'm walking on a bridge 200 feet high
I'm scared
Not confident at all
              I fall...
    I'm falling...
        I'm falling?
            I'm falling!!!!!
Is someone there to catch me?
My conscience breathes
Waking me to an early five AM morning
  Wondering... is this another night of vanity's fear
  I walk toward the water undressing the approval I expect others to have of me
  I have no shame
  I am free of criticism
  Because I am me
  Even when I feel *am I Me?*

I breathe beyond

This flaw

Mind over matter says I no longer see

I fall in love with me

Music finds its way into our love and we engage

This bridge I no longer walk alone

Shake me upside down

I don't fall

I don't crawl

I'm not moved by vanity's presentation

I am free to love myself

The pavement becomes soft

Because I am fearless

No shame

No blame

Not tamed

Just free

Now my name is no longer I

It's we

And as we lie down

Free and I

Finally awake from fear's dream

Virgo's Loneliness

On the road day and night
No family
New flight
Loneliness
At its height
Career's growing
Living the life
Virgo, Virgo don't you know
While you're looking for people
There they go
Everyone loves you
Everyone adores you
Want to be near you
Would live for you

But you still feel alone

Analytical thoughts
Rummage your dome
Saying I'd rather be home

Your persistence
Explains that you must go on

Love invites
Its embrace into your life
You remember
How you paid the price
Being stepped on all night
This loneliness is false premonitions
Of your superstitious heart
Being afraid it will be torn apart
Seize those plots
And stop
Before those redundant stories start again
Zen
To agree with Virgo's soul homeliness
No more Virgo's loneliness

Reverie Dream

I'd given myself until my soul bled dry

Creating an idea of a perfect person

Hurting myself, turning love into a burden

They said love is patient

Love is kind

But what is love if it exists on one side?

Of the coin

Losing coins hoping for a better day

Live in your truth my dear darling

There's no manual

And this road is not solid

Call it

And live

Like Confucius did

Live the word of heaven

And you'll make it there

Play smart dear darling

Use your heart dear darling

But let your mind agree

That's when it's meant to be

Don't fret and digress

When you no longer feel a part of the pack

It's when you move for dolo

You really know where you're at

Comfort can create the illusion

You have time to waste

But to move daily with purpose

Is saying your grace

Give thanks to the moments that made you who you

are

Like the branches on the tree

You have infinite possibilities

Don't limit yourself to another being's mentality

Who they know or get to meet

Your journey is about YOU

Glide smooth across the maroon

and know YOU are all you can lose

Destination

Actions are a multitude of accessories
We put on and take off
Through time
Developing ourselves

Growth comes not with age
But with openness to the unknown

Insecurities are bricks
That can be turned into steps or a wall
It's up to us which way it builds

It takes experience to speak in love's confidence
Word of mouth is inexperience
thinking about the definition of love
Real love is in motion and wouldn't have time
to define itself

Nor create conditions
Love is an escapade on the arrival
of a non-stop flight through life
Believe in you
So, you can believe in me
And maybe one-day love can stay
to complete a future of us

Pain is necessary to give us strength to grow
Having the wherewithal to move on from pain spiritually
Is the actual conquest
We all have to work to get through
By truly loving thyself
We will be able to grow from the necessities
pain brings us to carry throughout life
What our emotion consists of
within our endeavors
our outcome is written from
Congruent figures seam together
like anger in a conversation with stubborn minds
The only absolute is the fact that change is constant

Confidence

I think I'm too good
think I'm better than the rest.
Confidence misunderstood
I just want to be my best.
Ashamed of what I love
result in hating
and depriving myself
of what might be good for me.
I am life
I refuse not to live what I am.
So, I am too good.
Too good for ignorance.
too good for the insolence.
Thank you for showing me
the difference between
fear and confidence.
One day,

hopefully
you'll see the light,
and I'll be waiting for you smiling
on the other side.

Empty Meets Free

The very thing that makes us strong can be what holds us from our happiness. The bridges we build up to shield our precious hearts are the same bridges hindering us from crossing the threshold of pain and growth. It's inevitable for us to be bruised, but only through those bruises do we heal and learn what type of skin we have.

Fear, the very thing that takes days away from our lives. The soul stealer, the happiness abandoner. Fear stems from rejection or lack of confidence. It should be a sin to contain so many inhibitions, reserved minds on the verge of a collision with insanity. A circle of mental anguish or complacency to end up with another lifetime of uncertainty, insecurities, and calamity.

Can we base our emotions on what we feel and not on the premeditated outlook we pose as our feelings based on our upbringing and assimilation to social constructs? Even though we are blessed and privileged, we can be so sad inside. A reoccurring emotion reembraces itself into our lives very often and we can't seem to find what is missing, leaving us unhappy.

It feels like we're emotionally alone. Like we have no one that gets us or even wants to. This creates feelings of incompetence and loneliness, and feeling misunderstood. Maybe we put ourselves out there to be a crutch for others and make them so dependent we don't get anything out of it.

The reality is that the only thing we can change in this world is our self. With each problem, the solution is going to be internal changes to accommodate where we would like to be or feel. The only power we have is to change the way we perceive our interactions and deal with the life we are creating with our agreements. The core and the result is understanding the alchemy of life which is our choice in everything we engage in on a day-to-day basis.

Love is to Blame, Faith is its Dame

Pulse beating in hand

intensity tripling

Simplify human connection

unnumbered chances to a level unknown

Humility I'm prone

Humility becomes my noun

Humility becomes my now

Explain the etymology

Scientifically speak

How ether can create such

A love with peace

Giving me an answer

That doesn't include my mind

Which is prime

But can't calculate adrenaline

I know it's not my stomach

What I feel is an everlasting rock in my chest
Near my left breast
And it's repeating this beating
Noise the substance
I can't seem to tame
Love is to blame
Faith is its dame

The God Within

No one teaches us both the rationale and subconscious nature of our decisions

We just know to feel our way through life's bridges

Touching one another with our openness and gifts

Learning to be free and embrace all we were meant

To be, or not is what we regard forever

Lost in the sauce of how sauce should taste never guessing

That your recipe can be unique

Something to spread to your brethren

Yet we live life through theology based on a written heaven

Never thinking if we seek within God may start speaking

Gaining keys and jewels

Products to be used on a journey of completion

Distracted by what was, is, and should be on the daily

Mind locked like the center of a clock waiting for the next Alex Haley

So, excuse me if I retort my madness in the midst of my gifts unraveling

I am MY I am so I brand myself with love like a casualty battling

Seeking an intelligent way to discern my emotions

And balance with my spirit mixing quotients with potions

Of words that speak life

I am A complex anomaly guiding my inner light

Athena

A consoler of hearts
A controller of minds
Her vision is art
No one can define
Athena, Athena
The wisdom, God's light
Athena, Athena
The giver of life

The challenger of verbs
The beauty with words
Like a free bird
Confidence that sings the song
Of nature's bones
Athena, Athena
No color, the name, the sun
Athena, Athena

The heavenly goddess of wisdom

Break temptation with reason
Making saints out of heathens
Healing minds that are diseased with
False truth, Life breathing
Athena, Athena
Queen stands up to the name
Athena, Athena
Forever children of the universe will crave

The Essence of a Mesmerizing Earth

Knowledgeable Athena

Supreme Queen

Earth Dragon

Living Mood Ring

Vivacious Brooklyn

Brownstone stoop-cooking

Simply complicated

Constantly creating

Depth variation moving and shaking

She breathed the same air

Live in a shell designed the same

But what makes a difference

Is that what one decides

To do

The majority becomes a minority report

Of how to effectively turn negative

Into positive protective liberation

Possessing the art of building wisdom to live within

Digital with a free mind

Building the good in self

And watch it spread like fire

To live in 100% harmony

She was conceived to do it

Remain here from current life until next

Spoken to any mesmerizing Earth

This time I'm standing up

For those who handed their birth right to righteousness

Karmic stability and emotional intelligence

Will be the guide throughout life

This is just a reminder for the future Earths to see

That what you're looking for in life is waiting patiently

in you and me

Affirmations

Gratitude

I'm happy with my life,

I'm just frustrated with this moment,

that will be gone in a second.

Collaboration

My Dream's reality

is determined by my mind and willpower.

I am all that I see in my future.

I support the universe as it supports my growth.

I am powerful, open and flexible to an abundant future.

Cup Full of Openness

Today as I awake,

I premeditate positivity and success within my day.

I accept abundant and fruitful interactions.

I also accept the need to be fluid and flexible

with changes that may come my way.

I can and will find a conducive reason

for everything I encounter.

Virtues of Joy

Today I acknowledge

I am positively overwhelmed with abundance.

I am abundant.

I will freely give out blessings of good energy

and life-filled communication.

I will spread my greatness by smiling

at each person I encounter

and acknowledging their presence

with a warm and joyful greeting.

Unconditional Love and Regard

I seek love and consideration in my life,

So, I will give love unconditionally to myself and others.

The love that radiates within me

Will attract others who seek the same unconditional regard

And love within them and others.

I will be kind to myself and others.

I will speak highly of myself and others.

I will positively affect change in my life,

And attract others on the same path

Of unconditional love and high self-regard.

Attitude of Gratitude

I have changed my attitude toward

Life and what I encounter in my life.

I know by making these changes

I will develop an appreciation for experiences.

I know the greatness I seek in my life

Must first occur in my mind and speech.

I speak life into my day and will discipline my mind

To achieve joy and appreciation.

I am a part of what is great in the world.

Being grateful for my presence, talents, and life will

Send good vibes out and back to me.

I am grateful for my journey and where I am headed in my life.

All I Do is Win

I am aware that most winners

Win due to consistency, perseverance,

And regarding "no" as "not yet" or "not here".

I am mentally strong and capable

Of enduring tests and will prove

I deserve the abundance and

Prosperity I seek by staying the course, being open

flexible.

Honor Thyself

Today I honor myself by doing

What I say I'm going to do.

I will complete all tasks placed

On my to-do-list and not overthink

Experiences I am supposed to learn from.

If I think it and speak it, I shall do it.

Managing Karma

I understand I am responsible for my life

Experiences through karma.

With this fact, I will purposefully do good by those I encounter.

I will communicate properly.

I will change my assumptions to questions.

I will change my discomfort into laughter.

I take responsibility for my place in life.

I will grow this aspect of myself daily.

I will manage my own karma by being aware

Of my actions and thoughts toward myself and others.

Self-Preservation is Peace

Today I place into practice

The preserving of my time and energy.

I openly accept the replenishment of my energy,

By taking charge

When I need to be recharged.

I will protect my energy.

I respect my own time.

I am valuable,

And so is my time and energy.

Yoga and Meditation

I stretch my body and release

My thoughts,

Feelings,

Stress and energy

From yesterday.

I will allow yoga and meditation

To be catalysts for daily

Transformation and release.

I Love Myself

I love myself

So much,

Others will have no choice but to follow suit.

I am the prototype and example

For the type of love

I desire to receive, starting with unconditional love

From me to me.

I am beauty,

Light,

Love,

And a child of the most high.

My love is abundant for me.

I allow others to abundantly love me as well.

Learn To Let it Go

I acknowledge any discomfort I feel

As an attachment

I have not addressed internally.

I have identified or will identify

What is truly bothering me and address it.

I am at the core of all my feelings

And accept the changes I am making

To better myself and my thoughts.

I accept responsibility for what I continuously think about.

I agree to form a better ritual of thinking

As I hear my thoughts throughout the day.

Moral Compass

My moral compass

Is my governing tool though life.

I will continue to cultivate and listen

To it.

By doing so,

I will stay aligned with my journey

And lead my actions

With my morals and values.

Sunshine

i open the windows

of my heart

and allow

the prism of life

to shine all over me today.

Relationship With Peace

Today

I ditch my relationship

with fear and perfection.

I pick up my relationship with

meditation and effort creating internal peace.

Self-Love

To receive love

I'll change my actions and thoughts

toward love.

Looking outside myself

will leave love

outside of me.

If I look within

I can identify and radiate

the love I desire.

Acknowledgments

This book is dedicated to my daughters Jaira Jazzelle and Serenity Marie. You both are the perfect reason to get up in the morning. I am humbled by your presence. Life truly began when you both became a part of my life and journey. Your smile can light a room in the dark.

To Pride and Fear:

My will would not be as strong if I had not encountered you two. I have peace and happiness in my life after our relationship so I thank you for your guidance and push. I now know what company I do not desire to keep.

Lastly, to all my Mesmerizing Earths: the dreamers turned believers turned doers. We are all inspiration for one another's growth. Don't be afraid to reach out and learn from those who inspire you.

This book is well over ten years old but I am grateful to be putting it out today. It means so much to me.

About the Author

Q.B. Wingfield is a mother, writer, health and wellness advocate, entrepreneur, intellectual property educator and consultant.

What does it mean to grow into an adult, finding yourself and your path in life? Quyionah "Brooklyn" Wingfield has been through the love, pain, and beauty of young womanhood. With her own unique voice, she blazes a path for others to follow, helping them help themselves.

Wingfield draws her hypnotic writings from music and nature, two of her greatest inspirations. This visionary author, entrepreneur, intellectual property management educator, and mother of two daughters fought hard to earn her wisdom and strength. In "The Essence of a Mesmerizing Earth" she shares her enlightening insight with the wider world.

www.ingramcontent.com/pod-product-compliance
Lightning Source LLC
Chambersburg PA
CBHW071630080526
44588CB00010B/1342